DATE DUE

Fortiner, Virginia J.
    Science-hobby book
of archaeology
                    B 27-872

Science-Hobby Book of
Archaeology

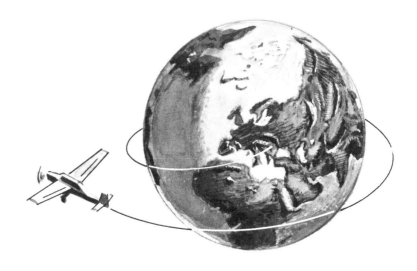

Science-Hobby Book of
Archaeology

by

VIRGINIA J. FORTINER

FOREWORD BY

JOSEPH V. NOBLE
Vice-Director for Administration
THE METROPOLITAN MUSEUM OF ART
NEW YORK CITY

Published by
LERNER PUBLICATIONS COMPANY
Minneapolis, Minnesota

CONTENTS

Second Printing 1971

Revised edition copyright© 1968 by Lerner Publications Company
Original copyright© MCMLXII by Hammond Incorporated

International Standard Book Number: 0-8225-0552-5
Library of Congress Catalog Card Number: 68-54177

Manufactured in the United States of America

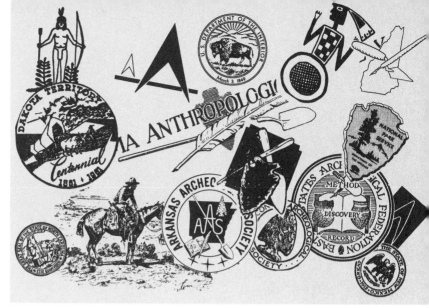

Acknowledgments

Many people have kindly assisted in person and by correspondence in the preparation of this brief and informal introduction to archæology, especially Edward Hunter Ross, Curator of Ethnological Collections of the Newark (N.J.) Museum, who took an interest in the idea of the book from the beginning, read the manuscript, and was ever generous with helpful suggestions.

I am very grateful to Dr. John L. Cotter, Region Five Archæologist of the National Park Service; Gladys Davidson Weinberg, Editor of *Archæology;* Edward Bacon, Archæology Editor of *The Illustrated London News;* Dr. Frederick J. Dockstader, Director of the Museum of the American Indian Heye Foundation; Joseph V. Noble, Operating Administrator of the Metropolitan Museum of Art; Herbert C. Kraft, Curator of the Seton Hall University Museum, South Orange, N. J.; Louis F. Ismay, Director of the Rensselaer County Junior Museum, Troy, N. Y.; and Marvin E. Tong, Jr., Director of the Museum of the Great Plains, Lawton, Okla.

For their cooperation on the amateur youth survey, I am particularly indebted to Dr. Joffre L. Coe, President of the Eastern States Archæological Federation and these state representatives:

Arkansas: Charles R. McGimsey, III, State University Museum, Fayetteville

Colorado: Omer C. Stewart, State Archæological Society, State University, Boulder

Georgia: Prof. A. H. Kelly, State University, Athens

Indiana: Dr. Glenn L. Black, State Archæologist, State Historical Society, Indianapolis

Iowa: Dr. W. D. Frankforter, Sanford Museum and Planetarium, Cherokee

Kansas: Carlyle S. Smith, State University Museum, Lawrence

Louisiana: J. Ashley Sibley, Jr., Junior Archæological Society, Baton Rouge

Massachusetts: Maurice Robbins, Bronson Museum, Attleboro

Missouri: Dr. Carl H. Chapman, State University, Columbia

Montana: Mary K. Dempsey, State Historical Museum, Helena

New Jersey: Dorothy Cross, State Archæologist; Kathryn B. Greywacz, State Museum Director, Trenton

New Mexico: Dr. Bertha P. Dutton, Museum of New Mexico, Santa Fe
New York: Louis C. Jones, State Historical Association, Cooperstown
North Carolina: Conway Rose, State Archæological Society, Goldsboro
North Dakota: Norman Paulson, State Historical Society, Bismarck
South Dakota: Will G. Robinson, State Historical Society, Pierre
Tennessee: Dr. Alfred K. Guthe, State University, Knoxville
Texas: E. Mott Davis, State University, Austin
Utah: Gordon L. Grosscup, State University, Salt Lake City
Wisconsin: Mrs. Philip H. Weigand, State Archæological Society, Milwaukee

Also, I want to thank these persons: Hamilton Warren, Director of the Verde Valley School, Sedona, Ariz., Thompson Webb, Headmaster of the Webb School of California, Claremont; John Lander, instructor at St. Paul's School, Concord, N.H.; Marjorie Vetter of the staff of the Girl Scout magazine, *The American Girl,* and William S. Hillcourt, National Program Resources Director of the Boy Scouts of America.

Also Flora Bailey, anthropologist, author, and teacher; Kay Marvin of the Summit (N.J.) High School Library; Evelyn Forsyth Selby and Amy Vanderbilt; Helen V. D. Winter, Director of the Maplewood (N.J.) Memorial Library, Lorraine Stewart Fiske (who typed the manuscript), and my other associates on the Maplewood Library staff.

Lastly, one more thank you to "T.T." who has mastered, among other things, the art of breaking the barriers of time and space.

VIRGINIA J. FORTINER

Maplewood, N. J.

Edouard Alexandre Sain, the French Academician who painted "Excavators at Pompeii" in 1866, would be surprised to know it would appear as an example of amateurs helping out at digs. One expert believes it was based on photographs rather than the artist's romantic conception.

Art Department,
Newark Public Library

Foreword

The quest of archæology is all the more enticing because the answers to its questions lie buried in the ground around us waiting to be discovered. Every man-made object that is found carries within itself the clues as to who made it and when. It is the challenging task of the archæologist to find this evidence and to interpret it correctly.

Many outstanding archæologists have come from the ranks of the amateurs. Mycenae and Troy were discovered in the last century by the indomitable and self-educated archæologist, Heinrich Schliemann. Only recently the baffling Minoan-Mycenaean texts written in Linear Script B were brilliantly translated by Michael Ventris, another amateur.

An interest in archæology at an early age is an excellent beginning. As a boy I started by finding Indian arrowheads on my uncle's farm in southern New Jersey.

This book may motivate you to take an active interest in this fascinating subject. If it does, I suggest that you join with other amateurs and professionals in membership in the Archæological Institute of America whose main offices are at 5 Washington Square North, New York 3, N. Y. The Institute publishes two outstanding quarterly magazines: *Archæology,* for the general reader, and the *American Journal of Archæology,* a scholarly publication. Membership also includes affiliation in one of the fifty local societies situated in principal cities across the country, which hold monthly meetings and lectures. Write to the main office and inquire about a student membership, and if you are interested in the vocational possibilities also ask for the free pamphlet on the subject, *Archæology as a Career* by John Howland Rowe.

In archæology there are many new worlds to conquer, and now science has given us revolutionary new tools for the quest. I envy those of you who accept this great new challenge.

JOSEPH V. NOBLE
Vice-Director for Administration
THE METROPOLITAN MUSEUM OF ART
NEW YORK CITY

Joseph V. Noble

THE PARTHENON: The glory that was Greece, the grandeur that is Archaeology.

Archæology is a great rough rock of a word that you can look at from many angles. From one angle, it is the world's most exciting and puzzling whodunit, a continued mystery story whose installments will appear as long as there is a Last Man on this planet. From another angle, it is the search for more information on your great-great-grandfather to the Nth degree, all the way back to the First Man on this planet. And from still another point of view, it is the best machine we have here and now to help us look backward into the dim reaches of time.

There are many, many definitions of this science-art, or art-science, but most of them are discouraging and involved. Perhaps the most satisfying — and certainly the simplest — was coined by Stanley Casson in his *Progress of Archæology:* "Archæology is the study of the human past, concerned chiefly with the activities of man as a maker of things."

Until about the middle of the last century, it was more of a hobby than a profession, and the amateurs who practiced it were more interested in art history — *antiquities* — than in science. *Artifacts* (as we call all man-made objects) were collected because they were beautiful, valuable, curious, or all three at once. As for fossils, who but a man as wise as Leonardo da Vinci suspected the story they would someday tell us?

Ever since they began farming, men have saved the sharpened pieces of flint or chert (prehistoric tools and weapons), they came across while working in the fields. But even a couple of generations ago, a farmer would have been amazed to hear that his "curiosities," stored somewhere around the house, were actually little clues to the mystery of ancient man.

Oddly enough, that news would have been a shock to ancient man himself! As one of today's great British archæological writers, Stuart Piggott, reminds us:

> "Prehistoric flint implements, or Roman pottery, or Medieval churches were not thought of as historical evidence by the men who made them, but they acquire the nature of evidence when the archæologist discovers, examines and interprets them."

Suppose, then, that we think of the archæologist as the investigator who must *discover, examine,* and *interpret* the clues; the leader of the search; the inventor and operator of what amounts to a science-fiction time machine . . . If he ends up by sounding like a superman, too important to be bothered by ordinary mortals, that means we are forgetting his basic approach: an archæologist is more interested in life than in death; in people, than in things.

Mythological figures and scenes from everyday life are combined in the paintings on this red-figured hydria, or water jar.

THE THRILL OF FINDING

Just as you are thrilled to find an arrowhead, the archæologist is excited to make an important discovery, whether beautiful, valuable, curious, or all three at once. But all the while he is concentrating his attention on something invisible.

He looks for and studies an object in order to learn more about the *man* who made it and the way that *man* lived, whether in Colonial Williamsburg or in the caves of Lascaux.

As a scientist, he is an extremely busy person, so absorbed he may seem withdrawn, and his special language is mystifying (except for his strange pleasure in referring to his excavations as digs!). Although studying the past, he is wide-awake to the modern world, and today he welcomes the interest and help of the sincere and intelligent amateur.

Why today, especially? That's one of those cause and effect questions. Whether professionals now feel more kindly toward amateurs because the amateurs are becoming more professional in *their* attitude, or whether the willingness of some enlightened professionals to give of themselves by guiding amateurs has borne fruit . . . who knows? The fact remains that amateur archæology of a high order is growing ever more popular in America today.

THE NEXT DECADES

Within the next ten or twenty years, this author believes, amateur archæology will have attained in this country the status long since won in England. There are so many earnest hobbyists in the British Isles, that radio and television not only devote regular programs to this subject but have actually been known to help finance real digs!

No longer just a collecting hobby to play at in spare time, it is now recognized as an avocation with an appeal so challenging that all kinds of people actually want to work at it.

All over this country, thousands of amateurs, ranging in age from junior high school students to retired business and professional people, are bringing a new vitality to the archæological or historical societies of their home states. They are gladly devoting many hours to learning those fundamental techniques that transform a volunteer from a liability to an asset in the field. In the laboratories of museums and universities, they are being taught how to sort, label, clean, catalog, exhibit, and sometimes restore the artifacts recovered by excavation.

Once they are trained to observe with scientific accuracy, they can alert professionals to significant sites. This was done most dramatically in Alabama where the famed Russell Cave, inhabited by prehistoric Indians almost 10,000 years ago, was first discovered by amateurs of the Tennessee Archæological Society.

To the amateur, all this adds up to fun, regardless of how difficult a "hobby" it may seem at first glance. And no amateur is more enthusiastic than the teen-ager, with his curiosity, enjoyment of outdoor life, and unspoiled talents for observation. This holds true whether he lives in the West — which we think of as real "Indian country" — or any other part of the United States.

To the professional, rightly on guard against the *treasure seeker* (or "pothunter," as he calls the digger who destroys the clues while collecting

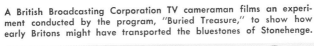

A British Broadcasting Corporation TV cameraman films an experiment conducted by the program, "Buried Treasure," to show how early Britons might have transported the bluestones of Stonehenge.

Paul Johnstone, BBC Television

the loot), this means recognizing a *truth seeker* when he sees one. This newcomer is the friend and helper for whom he has long hoped. Someone who shares his attitude toward the past and who, like himself, cares more about *conserving than collecting, finding out than finding.*

The coming of age of amateur archæology in America has been partly in response to a great emergency — the salvage situation. This is a world-wide problem but nowhere is it more acute than in this, most "progressive" of nations, because as we are building for the future, we are destroying our own past! Wherever earth-moving machines are at work on vast construction projects, irreplaceable evidence, we cannot afford to lose, is being wiped forever from the slate.

The greatest danger comes from the flood control and irrigation projects our government provides in answer to the water problems of its citizens. There is irony in this fact. The early Americans, like all peoples with primitive transportation, settled near great rivers or their tributaries because of their own water problems. So the river basin areas, being reclaimed for the sake of future generations, are the very places where the richest archæological remains are left from past generations!

In a race for time, in 1946, the Federal Government began, after extensive preliminary surveys, a drive to salvage or record evidence from such threatened sites. Since then it has endorsed the River Basin Salvage Program.

This miracle of our time is *without precedent in the world history of archæology.* The program's remarkable job of emergency excavations is due to the cooperation of the Smithsonian Institution in Washington, the National Park Service, and a committee of outstanding archæologists. These three groups, in turn, have enlisted the aid of museums, universities, archæological and historical societies from the whole country. All united to "save our sites." State governments, too, have contributed their share to the emergency operation.

Priority was given the Missouri River Basin, where over 100 reclamation projects were scheduled to change the face of this significant area. Here the salvage crews sometimes just managed to keep ahead of the flood waters.

By the end of 1961, 5 million specimens including paleontological, or fossil remains had been recorded at 10,000 sites. Recordings in words and pictures had been made of the material that could not be salvaged, such as rock paintings. These sites ranged from prehistoric villages and burial grounds to fur-trading posts, forts, and pioneer settlements on the frontier. They were located in 300 reservoir areas in nine-tenths of the states.

Dr. John O. Brew, director of the Peabody Museum of Archæology and Ethnology at Harvard and an internationally known authority on salvage archæology, wrote in 1961, ". . . when one views the River Basin studies . . . it is seen that archæology has progressed at a rate which would not have been likely during many decades or perhaps even a century of sporadic digging."

Let us hope this is only the first of such miracles. The 1954 experiment of New Mexico in saving sites along the path of new highways is being tried in other states; the National Park Service is restoring Philadelphia's Inde-

These items are artifacts salvaged by River Basin teams at Fort Pierre II, S.D.

pendence Square section in cooperation with an urban renewal plan; industry is giving archæologists the chance to "get in a few licks" where pipelines and power lines are being laid. Who knows where it will all end?

Running like a bright thread through the official reports of the River Basin Program are tributes to amateurs "without whom we could never have accomplished what we did." Why is this help so essential? Because the total force of professional American archæologists numbers only about 4,000 — and a large number of these are specialists in other countries. Some of these are specialists in research fields and never dig at all. The archæologist is not always a man with a spade.

YOUTH IN THE FIELD

Teen-agers are in the vanguard of those serving in the ranks to preserve our past. When an informal national survey of their contributions to amateur archæology was made, reports from many states showed that young people are making a real contribution to salvage projects. A curator of a Kansas museum and officers of the Missouri Archæological Society were enthusiastic about the work of teen-agers as volunteers at digs in the vital Missouri River Basin area.

Another friend of youth, North Carolina Society President, Conway F. Rose, had as his 1962 goal the training of amateurs — with emphasis on juniors — in the fundamentals of the science. He hopes, eventually, "to field a small army of young folks capable of contributing a great deal to archæology." Two 15-year-old members did such a splendid job in North Carolina on the Roanoke River salvage project in 1961 that they were asked to return the next summer vacation.

New Jersey pioneered with an unusual educational experiment in 1961 when forty junior and senior high school students from Roxbury spent six weeks of their vacation in fieldwork along the Delaware River in a section due to be flooded for the Tocks Island Reservoir. Sparked by an appeal by State Archæologist, Dorothy Cross, to save Lenni Lenape Indian sites, the project was planned by a science teacher, Karl Brecheisen, and a history teacher, Bennet Satz. It was approved by the local Board of Education as a non-tuition, non-credit summer enrichment course.

Class members studied excavation techniques with a field director from Columbia University; their teachers had been trained earlier by Dr. Cross at Hunter College. They loved their work at the digs — and at the Trenton State Museum on rainy days — as much as those swims in the river on hot afternoons. Said one young girl to a newspaper reporter, "There is a lot of excitement connected with past history, and archæology makes it come alive. Field trips are fun, and I like being outdoors while learning about the Indians and how they lived."

In most states, the survey showed, teen-agers are playing an active part as junior members of the state societies. In at least three, New Mexico, Louisiana, and Texas, they have formed their own clubs with adults as advisers or auxiliary members.

Most of the responses to the survey came from adults, but 16-year-old Jerry Brown of the Lovington Junior Archæological Society in New Mexico sent one of the best letters on file. "Being a junior organization automatically

A junior member of the Massachusetts Archaeological Society and her father, and three Girl Scouts work at Wapanucket #6, prehistoric Indian village site. Dr. Maurice Robbins, curator of the museum, led amateurs who discovered and dug this significant site.

Bronson Museum,
Attleboro, Mass.

University of Texas

Austin Junior High students excavate a 5-foot square in the Gatewood Rock Shelter, Austin.

The Newark (N.J.) News

Two salvage workers from the Roxbury (N.J.) High School with their find of a Lenni Lenape Indian hoe on a Delaware River site.

Volunteer diggers excavate an Archaic period site. This State Archaeological Society includes a mailman, a psychiatrist, a salesman, a professor, and a farmer. Note grid pattern measured off with string.

Sanford Museum, Cherokee, Iowa

These Ute boys, direct descendants of the first Americans, are curious about their ancestors, too. With them is Curator Gordon L. Grosscup (center) of the University of Utah Museum at a reservation dig.

Community Services, Fort Duchesne, Utah

Archaeologists' tools against the background of a portable screen for sifting soil.

classifies us as 'just a bunch of kids,' " he writes, "but this is something we are constantly trying to rectify. Our goals and principles are the same as professionals. Our members are given instruction in the correct methods of excavating, recording, preservation, etc. The greatest unpardonable sin to us is vandalism and improper excavation. Actually, this business of being on our toes and proving ourselves . . . keeps us alert and interested."

Jerry describes the appeal of archæology for his generation very eloquently: "The main reason the more dedicated members like archæology is that it links them with the past. Out hunting or on a site, we can see firsthand the tools and other artifacts with which ancient man worked and lived. We can feel and imagine his struggle for existence, for life itself.

"Actually, all this seems to challenge us to attempt to answer the baffling questions: What was this artifact used for? Why did the Indians leave this part of the country?"

These junior and senior high school students, including both boys and girls, have been guided by members of the Hobbs (N.M.) Archæological Society. They expect to stick on the job for a couple of years, as patiently as real "pros" at their Indian village site where each one takes responsibility for a 3-foot-wide trench. Such demonstration of youth's *dedication, curiosity, and the drive to find answers is significant. For this is the essence of archæology!*

In Louisiana and Texas, other young people have formed independent societies. An inspiring example is set by the Baton Rouge Junior Archæological Society. This group of boys was organized in 1960 as a result of the enthusiasm of a social science teacher, Zilda P. Sibley, for amateur archæology and Indian lore. The society boasts its own bus for expeditions, a special library and museum in the Walnut Hills School, a newsletter, and a fine motto: Knowing the Past Betters the Future.

The following are newsworthy items on this society's crowded program:

classes in both archæological techniques and Indian handicrafts; detailed reports on digs; interviews with Indians on a nearby reservation which have been taped and photographed; trips to historic sites, museums, and universities over a wide area; and lectures by faculty members and graduate students from the Louisiana State University. Members share all finds with the University and the Archæological Society of Louisiana, their "big brother" associates.

In Austin, Texas, a group of junior high students attend classes given by the City Recreation Department and work at sites with students from the University of Texas. They have formed a club. Already, according to E. Mott Davis, a research scientist and lecturer at the University, they are "developing into reasonably knowledgeable archæologists." Mr. Davis also has the opportunity to assess the contribution of older teen-agers and reports that they are in the "core group" of hard workers in the organization. What's more, some of them even persuade their parents to join and get to work, too!

In both the Southeast and the Southwest amateur archæology is one of the Girl Scouts' most popular and successful activities. What started out as a local Girl Scout project in Mobile, Alabama in 1957, soon spread throughout that state and is now being actively — and happily — carried on in the four other states of the national organization's "Dixie Region" namely, Arkansas, Louisiana, Mississippi, and Tennessee. The pattern set in Mobile, where members received training from experts at the Alabama Museum of Natural History and Mound State Monument at Moundville before going out on field trips, has been consistently followed. The girls were made to feel they must measure up to the professionals' standards — and they did. Incidentally, they have nicknamed this project "Archy"!

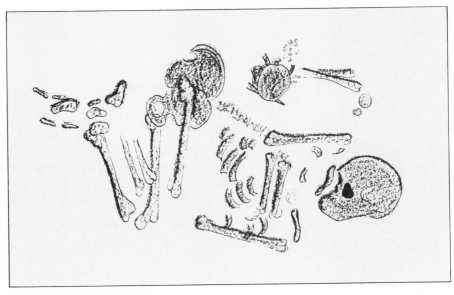

Indiana History Bulletin

Archaeologists' children sometimes join the team. This sketch of a flexed burial with votive offerings was made by Ellen MacLean, a teen-ager, when her father, J. Arthur MacLean, was making the first scientific excavation of Albee Mound in Indiana.

The girls are making interesting finds. At a dig on the shore of Mobile Bay, they excavated a shell *midden* (a mound formed of shells discarded by seafood-eating Indians over a long period). These Indians, they discovered, had sometimes used clay balls instead of heated rocks and pebbles for their cooking, a method previously observed only in excavating middens made by Western tribes.

The intense interest of Southwestern Scouts stems largely from the influence and "contagious enthusiasm" of one woman, Dr. Bertha P. Dutton, a curator of the Museum of New Mexico at Santa Fe. For many years, Dr. Dutton led field expeditions of Scouts and other girls throughout New Mexico and neighboring states and worked with them at the museum, one of this area's most important centers for the study of Indian cultures.

Some of her "alumnæ" were so absorbed that they went on to become either archæologists or anthropologists. One of them, Nettie Adams is now assisting her husband, an archæologist assigned to the Aswan Dam salvage project in Egypt. Mrs. Adams, a native of Oklahoma, spent her first summer with Dr. Dutton's group at the age of fifteen and decided to make anthropology her career.

This happens to boys, too. The Wisconsin Archæological Society, for example, takes pride in several former junior members who entered the profession. Several members of Indiana's Trowel and Brush Society, a professional organization of young archæologists, who were trained at Angel Mounds, began as teen-age hobbyists.

Teen-agers made a significant contribution in excavating a 200-year-old fort at Crown Point, N.Y. L. F. Ismay, Rensselaer Museum director led Boy Scouts and others in the 5-year project, which culminated in the purchase and restoration of the site by experts.

Rensselaer County Junior Museum, Troy, N. Y.

18

"Anybody can dig up things; but it is only by observation and interpretation that we can dig up the past."

— *Sir Leonard Woolley*

The artifacts of modern man — complex and delicate devices that have developed from his discoveries in physics, nuclear research, even space exploration — are helping today's archæologist to find and interpret the artifacts of ancient man, those simple tools with which the cycle of technology began.

Like the automative devices in our factories, offices, and homes, the new tools are providing shortcuts, saving precious time for the student of the long reaches of the past, who has only the short span of the present at his disposal.

Although, like all new inventions, they are still costly to produce and operate, these devices are money saving in the long run. The large-scale excavations going on continually over the entire globe require much money and many men. It would take an electronic computer to estimate the man-hours of research that precede and follow such expeditions.

"The particular skill of Sherlock Holmes," says biographer Leon Edel, ". . . lay not so much in observing the bits of mud on the boots of the visitor . . . or reading between the lines of what he was saying. It lay in his power of deduction, his imaginative grasp of his materials, his ability to deduce the unknown from the known."

Here is an exact parallel to the investigator's secret of examining and interpreting the evidence he has discovered. And at every step of the way, from discovery through interpretation, brother scientists are now offering him their assistance.

The archæologist has learned that great centers of population are never in arid deserts or on snowy mountaintops — uncomfortable places! — but are usually found in fertile river valleys. As of today, he believes that the "cradle of civilization" was in the valleys of the Tigris, Euphrates, and Indus Rivers, but tomorrow — who knows? Because he is now interested in the total picture, the complete story of civilization's unfolding, he is thinking not in terms of individual states but in links between peoples. He continues the archæological tradition of "checking up" on history and legends. At the same time, he keeps on pushing back the barriers of time in the search for still earlier ancestors. For all these reasons, and because of the fine new tools he has acquired, he often reworks old sites and reassesses old finds, while simultaneously carrying on the search for new ones.

The discovery of new sites stems mainly from intensive and exhaustive research in broad spheres of knowledge but, like a good detective, the archæologist never underestimates the value of two less predictable factors: observations reported by the public and his own intuitive reasoning. Any day, from Mesopotamia to Missouri, "chance finds" of potsherds or projectile points, fossils, or bones may signalize an important discovery. Both professional reports and popular writings of archæologists are studded with sparkling examples of "hunches" that led to triumph. The true investigator can "read" the message of mounds that are not natural formations but have been built up by generations of men who chose the same spot — because it was near fresh water, or in a good defensive position, or just pleasant — as their temporary or permanent living place. He knows that, correctly excavated, these mounds will eventually reveal a succession of *occupation levels,* the rubbish and rubble of these generations, with the latest at the top and the oldest at the bottom. This rule, called *stratigraphy,* is true the world over, and it applies to places of burial as well.

Since stratigraphy stems from the geological rule of stratification of soil and rock, it could be called science's first gift to archæology. It was, in fact, discovered in 1784 by an American amateur geologist. His name? Thomas Jefferson! Although he "recorded" his experimental excavation of an Indian burial mound (or *barrow*), as all good archæologists should, it lay forgotten in his *Notes on the State of Virginia* until scientific archæology was born late in the last century. Belatedly the title of "first scientific digger" has been added to Jefferson's many other honors, by Sir Mortimer Wheeler noted for his own excavation technique.

Stratigraphy is most dramatically illustrated in the salvage archæology of a great metropolis. Londoners, before rebuilding after the blitz bombing of World War II, dug down through historic levels, past evidence of the Great Fire, past medieval monuments, to the Roman level where they found such undreamed of treasures as a beautiful temple, dedicated to an ancient "mystery religion," Mithraism.

HOW DOES MODERN SCIENCE SHOW LOCATION?

Next to a globe with a magic gimmick that says, "Dig here!" the nearest things to an archæologist's dream are the amazing new surveying methods that help pinpoint finds on a known site and the use of air reconnaissance photography which discloses new sites unrecognizable from the ground.

THREE CHIEF NEW SURVEYING METHODS:

1. *Electrical Resistivity:* Four metal rods or probes are inserted into the soil at a series of stated intervals across a site, and an electric current is passed between them. The drier the soil, the greater the resistance. Meter readings transferred to a graph will show clearly the lines of buried ditches or walls.

2. *Magnetic Surveying:* This makes use of a device known as the proton magnetometer, which discovers the patterns of magnetic variation across the areas surveyed. Interpreted by a technique used for guided missiles and computers, it reveals possible occupation evidence beneath the surface. The method was discovered in an Oxford University laboratory. It is being used in this country by state archæologist, Dr. Glenn A. Black of Indiana.

3. *Seismic Surveying:* A method employed by oil companies for the past twenty years to find salt domes and oil deposits, this is still an unwieldy and complicated procedure. It involves setting off a charge of dynamite and measuring the sound waves from the concussion as they are reflected back from various levels above and below bedrock. An instrument records the number of feet from the explosion where something, other than bedrock, is buried.

Within the next few years, the seismic and other experimental techniques will doubtless be improved and made more practical for archæological use. Portable proton magnetometers and resistivity machines already are available.

AIR RECONNAISSANCE TECHNIQUES

The incredible possibilities of site spotting from the sky were first recognized in 1900 by an Englishman, Dr. O. G. S. Crawford, and air surveys have been used to some extent ever since. But the perfection of air reconnaissance techniques in World War II are largely responsible for its present successful achievements. These include the use of infrared and ultraviolet filters, as well as new mapping instruments and cameras.

Although he rarely flies himself, aerial photography has given the archæologist wings. No longer earthbound, he can look into the heart of the jungle, observe caves deep in a mountainside, and peer down into the sea. Buried ruins, earthworks, mounds "camouflaged" with vegetation, roadways, even whole cities of the past become clear.

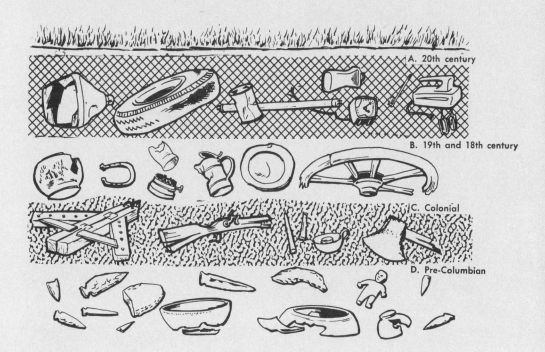

A. 20th century

B. 19th and 18th century

C. Colonial

D. Pre-Columbian

An artist's concept of stratigraphy. Will the plastic objects on our strata survive as future finds?

Only when photographed from the air were these concentric earthworks at Poverty Point (La.) Mound recognized as man-made rather than natural. Excavation confirmed air reconnaissance findings.

Mississippi River Commission, Corps of Engineers, U.S. Army, Vicksburg, Miss.

Viewed from above, inequalities on the ground and plant marks (variations in the height or color of the prevailing crop) are made visible by means of oblique and vertical shots. And these variations show, one way or another, the hand of man.

This technique's greatest success stories have been in England (because of the damp climate) and in Italy where airborne cameras first discovered Spina, the city built in 500 B.C. by the pre-Roman Etruscans, who are now a favorite subject for Mediterranean scholars.

Here, by a happy coincidence, large aerial and tiny underground cameras first collaborated. A periscope device, that works in reverse and shows to a man on the surface what is below him, has a light ray and camera attached at its base. When the mirror reflects something interesting, photographs can be shot. Thus with a minimum of time, effort, and expense, archæologists learned which Etruscan tombs to excavate.

UNDERWATER ARCHÆOLOGY

Besides gaining wings, the archæologist has now acquired fins! Underwater archæology, like aerial surveys, dates back, officially, to the early 1900's — if you don't count the centuries, when divers spotted and salvaged treasure on their own. It, too, owes new aids to military advances, such as the frogman's aqualung.

Underwater archæology, for all its scientific uses, can hardly avoid carrying on the antiquity-collecting tradition of early excavators on dry land. A noted art critic has described the Mediterranean Sea as the "richest museum." Think of what glory and grandeur must have been lost over all these years in its blue depths! From the first great modern find — a magnificent collection of Greek bronzes and marbles brought up from a sunken ship in the Tunisian port of Mahdia — to Jacques-Yves de Cousteau's latest amphora, all the beautiful things saved must be only a hint of what Neptune is still keeping under guard.

The romance of submarine archaeology is typified by these finds from a Spanish galleon wrecked off the Florida coast in 1733. Bermuda divers found the silver-and-emerald bishop's cross. The "pieces of eight" are from the collection of Robert I. Nesmith, author of "Dig for Pirate Treasure" and curator of Foul Anchor Archives.

Foul Anchor Archives, Rye, N.Y.

HOW DOES MODERN SCIENCE SHOW CHRONOLOGY?

To appreciate the answer to this question, you need some idea of the archæologist's dating, or *chronology,* system and his other ways of working. There are two kinds of chronology: anything which can be dated according to written records (history), whether it be a sword from Cæsar's Gallic Wars or a Minie Ball from the Civil War, is classed as *absolute chronology;* anything not authenticated by such records is classed as *relative chronology.*

The exact location of an artifact on its stratigraphic level may be a clue to its age, especially in the light of the knowledge, already built up, of its makers and their periods. As with objects found at the scene of a murder, it is also important to know what is found together, the relationship or *association* of objects unearthed on the same level. The technical name for this is *context,* and it is one of the chief reasons why archæologists worry about the harm an untrained digger can do.

The true significance of a discovery may depend on this one factor, as can be clearly seen from the story of two of the most famous sites in the history of American archæology — Folsom and Clovis, N.M. In 1927, paleontologists first discovered at Folsom the remains of prehistoric man's weapons of chipped flint, embedded in the clay surrounding the bones of a beast known to have been extinct for thousands of years. It was identified as *Bison taylori*. Did this indicate that human beings had been on this continent far longer than was then estimated? About ten years later, at Clovis, the answer came when archæologists found a hunter's projectile point actually embedded in the bones of his prey. As artifacts, these two types of ingeniously flaked points fluted or channeled so they could be fastened to the ends of arrow shafts, were important indications of early technological skill, but the real story they had to tell was the antiquity of their makers. This message might never have been revealed there if the New Mexico sites had first been spoiled by haphazard diggers or pothunters to whom *context* was meaningless!

Folsom   Clovis

It is an archæological axiom that all excavation is destruction because nothing can ever be replaced just as it was found beneath the surface of the soil. Therefore, it is vitally necessary to protect and record all kinds of evidence the expert is prepared to observe and assess: silt in alluvial soil, seeds, small animal bones, and such, that the untrained eye would miss. This means that besides the original topographic survey map, an essential preliminary for every dig, the carefully measured grid pattern, in which the site is divided by trenches, must be similarly mapped. Lastly, each find must be identified with its exact location level and square on the grid pattern.

Of course, precise records in graph, chart, and written (or log) form are also kept for the entire procedure; artifacts are photographed and perhaps sketched, *in situ* (as found), then carefully sorted, labeled, and preserved.

This three-dimensional recording system, like stratigraphy, was first developed by an amateur, Gen. Pitt-Rivers. His large-scale excavations of Roman barrows and earthworks on a great estate in southern England occupied his retirement years in the mid-nineteenth century. These were conducted with military zeal and modern efficiency in remarkable contrast to the "dilettante digs" of his day.

If an expert had to name the single type of find most meaningful as a clue to chronology and other kinds of information, he would be almost certain to answer "potsherds." Why? Because pottery, a cheap and almost universal commodity and one of the first products of man on the way to civilization, has high *survival value*. Fragile though it is, pottery lasts almost forever when it is broken into sherds and tossed on the world's rubbish heap. Sometimes even sherds as tiny as a thumbnail can tell a story. Sometimes they only "talk" after they are painstakingly sorted, pieced, and cemented together (begin at the base and work upwards toward the rim). The way pottery is decorated can reveal how people lived and their religious beliefs, as well as their progress in the arts. Mycenean ware scattered at 100 sites around the Mediterranean has helped scholars reconstruct the trade routes of these pre-classical Greeks. Pollen used to temper clay for a pot, when chemically analyzed, not only dated its early Syrian makers but revealed that they had cattle. This pollen had passed through the animals' digestive tract.

Besides pollen analysis, the natural sciences contributed two other dating methods. One, the *varve* system, originating in Scandinavia, is based on the count of the annual layers of silt in glacial lakes; the other, originating in the Southwest, is the application of *dendrochronology,* or tree ring dating, to timbers used by the Indians in their settlements. Both have strict time and geographical limitations.

What spurred other branches of science to help solve archæology's great problem of relative chronology? Man's ever growing curiosity about pre-history, that vast, dark cave of the past where there are no dates to illuminate the shadows, no nations, no leaders, only an unimaginably longline of "anony-mous peoples." Bit by bit, the new ways of dating evidence of our early ancestors are shedding light on these eras which, first divided into the Stone, Bronze, and Iron Ages, have since been broken down into a bewildering array of tongue-twisting "periods."

A staff member at Museum of the American Indian, New York, studies and painstakingly pieces together sherds to recreate prehistoric pottery.

THREE CHIEF NEW DATING METHODS:

1. *Carbon-14:* — Dr. Willard F. Libby's Nobel-prize-winning discovery is now familiar. It is based on the principle that the radioactive C-14 atoms, remaining in a sample of wood, charcoal, peat, shell, bone, grain, or cloth (in such rare cases as the wrappings of the Dead Sea Scrolls), indicate the time passed since the sample was removed from the carbon dioxide cycle or "died." This method, constantly being improved, has accomplished such dramatic feats of detection that it has been called the "atomic age sleuth."

2. *Thermoluminescence:* — This method appears capable of dating back many years farther than carbon-14. The technique is used chiefly for pottery and glass. When a sample is heated to about 800 degrees Fahrenheit, trapped electrons in the clay are released, and the amount of glow emitted is measured by a special tube: the greater the glow, the older the sample.

Metropolitan Museum of Art

Archaeologists frequently turn detective to expose forgeries. Joseph V. Noble, Metropolitan Museum of Art, proved by spectrographic means that three Etruscan terracotta warriors in the museum were creations of the 20th century, not masterpieces of the 5th century B.C. Manganese used in coloring them was unknown in classical times. In Rome, 1960, the last surviving forger confessed his part in the hoax perpetrated over 40 years before.

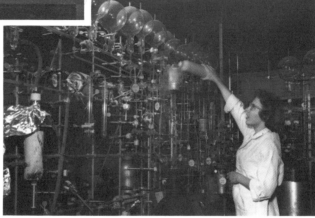

Isotopes, Inc., Westwood, N.J.

The gas preparation system is part of the intricate dating procedure in Carbon-14 laboratories. If more than 40,000 years old, the C-14 content is too low to be dated.

Dr. Bryant Tuckerman, with the aid of an electronic computer, compiled astronomical tables giving positions of the sun, moon, and planets for a 600-year period. This new dating method was compared with astronomical observations recorded on an ancient tablet to pinpoint the tablet's date. On the right is a magnetic tape storage reel.

International Business Machines Corporation

26

3. *Hydration of Obsidian:* — The rate, at which the edges and surfaces of this volcanic glass absorb moisture and form hydration layers, is a clue to the age of an obsidian object. It was used by prehistoric man for tools and weapons and, by later generations, for jewelry and other art objects.

Both dates and the origins of raw materials used in the making of glazed pottery and metal objects — including coins — are established by such techniques as *neutron activation* and *spectroscopy*. Such revelations not only open up whole new fields of research, (How did Bronze Age Britons obtain metal from Central Europe for their knives?), but help to expose those frauds and hoaxes which occasionally harass archæologists and museum directors.

In contrast to these comparatively short-range methods, *potassium argon,* outgrowth of carbon-14, can date rocks that are millions of years old. Thanks to this "atomic clock," the perennial and exciting discoveries of fossilized skulls and other human remains, by Dr. L. S. B. Leakey in the Olduvai Gorge of Tanganyika, can be given such incredible ages as 1,750,000 years. How? Through potassium argon testing of the volcanic rocks found *in association with* these fossils.

HOW TO BE AN AMATEUR ARCHAEOLOGIST

Amateur archæologists, like amateurs at anything, come in two styles: the armchair and the active. Archæology is an inclusive subject and can be fun from many angles. It draws people — like a magnet — from many directions; the wider their interests, the more archæology will hold them.

In some cases, people seem to have become amateur archæologists almost in spite of themselves. They never consciously chose it as a hobby at all. Maybe they started out by being interested in Indians, Greek art, speleology (cave exploration), local history, or skin diving. A brilliant career woman, who now spends every summer vacation at sites in Italy and Greece, says the bug bit her when she began studying classical writers for a course in *linguistics*.

Today, as we have seen, archæologists are marshaling to their aid specialists in many other branches of science. So it may become only a short step from the study of physics to the study of prehistory. Like other serious hobbyists, they soon find all conversational roads lead to their pet subject. Naturally, *they* know that archaeology is three-dimensional, taking in the whole world, past, present, and future. How can they help feeling sorry for people who have the fixed idea it is as dry as dust? Obviously, all good amateurs should get together! Someone has said that the great advantage of the amateur is that he need not specialize, like the professional. Certainly it is exciting to travel through time — on wings of books — from Colonial days to the Cro-Magnon period, and through space from our Midwest to the Middle East. But if you'd rather specialize — after looking over the field — there is satisfaction in becoming an expert yourself, however narrow your specialty.

Dr. John L. Cotter holds
a 17th-century wine bot-
tle against background
of a painting of a typi-
cal interior at James-
town (Va.) colony.

U.S. Department
of the Interior,
National Park Service

THOMAS JEFFERSON,
one of the first
amateur archaeologists

from a painting by
Rembrandt Peale,

New York Historical Society

This earth-moving machine,
once dreaded by archaeologists,
now proves efficient for preliminary excavation.

U.S. Department of the Interior,
National Park Service

AREAS ILLUSTRATING PREHISTORY AND THE INDIAN CULTURES

1. Aztec Ruins National Monument, N. Mex.
2. Bandelier National Monument, N. Mex.
3. Canyon de Chelly National Monument, Ariz.
4. Casa Grande National Monument, Ariz.
5. Chaco Canyon National Monument, N. Mex.
6. Effigy Mounds National Monument, Iowa
7. Gila Cliff Dwellings National Monument, N. Mex.
8. Hovenweep National Monument, Colo.-Utah
9. Mesa Verde National Park, Colo.
10. Montezuma Castle National Monument, Ariz.
11. Mound City Group National Monument, Ohio
12. Navajo National Monument, Ariz.
13. Ocmulgee National Monument, Ga.
14. Pipestone National Monument, Minn.
15. Tonto National Monument, Ariz.
16. Tuzigoot National Monument, Ariz.
17. Walnut Canyon National Monument, Ariz.
18. Wupatki National Monument, Ariz.
19. Yucca House National Monument, Colo.

AREAS ILLUSTRATING COLONIAL HISTORY

20. Ackia Battleground National Monument, Miss.
21. Cabrillo National Monument, Calif.
22. Castillo de San Marcos National Monument, Fla.
23. Colonial National Historic Park (Jamestown area), Jamestown National Historic Site, Va.
24. Coronado National Memorial, Ariz.
25. De Soto National Memorial, Fla.
26. El Morro National Monument, N. Mex.
27. Fort Caroline National Memorial, Fla.
28. Fort Frederica National Monument, Ga.
29. Fort Mantanzas National Monument, Fla.
30. Fort Necessity National Battlefield Site, Pa.
31. Fort Raleigh National Historic Site, N.C.
32. George Washington Birthplace National Monument, Va.
33. Gran Quivira National Monument, N. Mex.
34. San Jose Mission National Historic Site, Tex.
35. Tumacacori National Monument, Ariz.

AREAS ILLUSTRATING THE WAR FOR AMERICAN INDEPENDENCE

36. Colonial National Historic Park (Yorktown Battlefield area), Va.
37. Independence National Historic Park, Pa.
38. Morristown National Historic Park, N. J.

AREAS ILLUSTRATING POLITICAL AND MILITARY AFFAIRS 1783-1865

39. Chalmette National Historic Park, La.
40. Fort McHenry National Monument, Md.
41. Harpers Ferry National Monument, W. Va.-Md.

AREAS ILLUSTRATING THE ADVANCE OF THE FRONTIER AND WESTWARD EXPANSION

42. Chimney Rock National Historic Site, Nebr.
43. Fort Laramie National Historic Site, Wyo.
44. Fort Union National Monument, N. Mex.
45. Fort Vancouver National Monument, Wash.
46. Lava Beds National Monument, Cal.
47. Pipe Spring National Monument, Ariz.

AREAS ILLUSTRATING THE CIVIL WAR

48. Antietam Battlefield Site, Md.
49. Fredericksburg and Spotsylvania National Military Park, Va.
50. Gettysburg National Military Park, Pa.
51. Manassas National Battlefield Park, Va.
52. Petersburg National Military Park, Va.
53. Richmond National Battlefield Park, Va.
54. Shiloh National Military Park, Tenn.
55. Vicksburg National Military Park, Miss.

AREAS ILLUSTRATING COMMERCE, TRAVEL AND INDUSTRY

56. Grand Portage National Monument, Minn.
57. Hopewell Village National Historic Site, Pa.

Pre-Columbian clay figurines exhibited at the Museum of the American Indian.

A beautiful Greek amphora

Collection of the Newark Museum

The way you practice amateur archæology depends a great deal on where you live: city, country, North, South, East, or West. The popularity of archæology as a hobby in some sections was very neatly expressed by the South Dakota representative who answered the amateur survey. "Around here," he said, "most everybody is an amateur archæologist!" If you live in such an area, opportunities are boundless. For readers less fortunate — geographically speaking — here are a few suggestions:

1. Take out membership in your state archæological or historical society. Even if there is no local chapter, you might be able to attend a few statewide meetings at a nearby city. You will find its newsletters and other publications interesting and helpful; you will meet other amateurs and exchange information and ideas with them; you will have a chance to learn how to identify artifacts from studying private collections. If there is excavating going on in your state, you will hear about it. And, chances are, before long, you will want to take the next step, offer your services as a volunteer helper in the field or the lab and "get in there and dig."

2. Organize a club yourself in your community, school, or office with an archæologist as adviser. You'll probably be surprised to find how many others share your hobby and are glad you started the ball rolling. You're sure to be surprised — and stimulated — by the variety of their specialties.

3. Become a real gallery trotter at nearby museums, attend their lectures and programs, and make a point of including such visits in your plans when you travel. Most museum exhibits today are as modern and attractive as the window displays of a good department store, and you'll find yourself absorbing a lot of information in a pleasurable way. Study the labels and publications, too, and don't hesitate to ask questions. Museum staff members welcome visitors who are more than mere sightseers.

4. Become a site seer. Among the most fascinating sites to visit are the historic and prehistoric sites and restorations under the National Park Service. You will be given conducted tours by rangers who know everything there is to know about their subject and, better still, have been trained to

interpret the past rather than to instruct you about it. At the Park Headquarters you can browse through miniature museums that bring that area to life — for instance, on Civil War battlefields you get to the point where it would not surprise you to hear the rebel yell resounding outside the window!

5. Become a site spotter. You don't have to fly an airplane — or even drive a car — to make this important contribution of *alerting professionals to sites worth investigating*. In fact, it's one of the few modern activities that must be done on foot. The greatest asset for the site spotter, or any active amateur, is the same as for the professional, the power of *observation*. This presupposes curiosity and patience, for without curiosity, *why* would one observe; without patience, *how* could one observe?

Other advantages include: science hobbies — if you're a rock or shell collector, for instance, you have the habit of noticing what's underfoot; camping experience and knowledge of wood lore help you to be self-reliant in the great outdoors and appreciative of the Indians' solutions to their problems; photography, map making, drawing ability, and a knowledge of typing make it easier to record your finds in accurate style; lastly, like the "pro," you have an added asset if you are interested in science and history including the history of art, architecture, or technology. There is one other asset which, as a matter of fact, archæologists themselves usually put at the top of the list: interest in people, their likenesses and differences at all periods and throughout the world. This is not surprising when you remember that archæology is a branch of anthropology.

So you want to be a *site spotter?* Suppose there is an old iron furnace in your vicinity that you think has interesting possibilities. Here is your line of action:

a. Obtain all the information possible by reading about iron furnaces; go to your local library, even consult records at the county seat. Find out who built it, what was sold there, when it was abandoned, and what has happened there.

b. Write a report on what you have learned, both from your reading and observation of the site itself.

c. Survey the site in a professional way, perhaps even using surveyors' tools like an alidade and a plane table. Any good book on map making will tell you how.

d. Add the map to your dossier and send it to your local archæological or historical society, the anthropology department of the state university, or the state museum.

A similar procedure should be followed with Indian sites you discover or hear about from farmers who have found arrowheads, sherds, and artifacts. Read all you can on Indians, especially local tribes, and consult experts in Indian lore. When you are ready for action, you can save yourself trouble by checking first to see if your state conducts a county by county survey of its archæological features. In that case, more help from amateurs is always welcome, and there should be printed material available to guide them. If not, send for the Missouri Handbook No. 6, entitled *Indians and Archaeology*

Cave paintings

of Missouri, which is easily adapted to the needs of other areas. It is available from the Missouri Press, 103 Swallow Hall, University of Missouri, Columbia, Missouri for a reasonable price.

All through archæological history young people have shown themselves adept at site spotting. Caves, especially, seem to have an irresistible attraction for them. So many of the great prehistoric rock paintings and carvings have been uncovered due to such curiosity and daring that Norbert Casteret, the noted speleologist, once wrote a full-length article for *The National Geographic* in praise of the contributions of young people.

The five local boys, who crawled through a small hole, in 1959, in rocky country near Nerja, Spain, to discover a "subterranean wonderland," were each given a reward of about $500; three are now employed as guides for visitors to the Nerja caves.

In this country, government bounties have not yet materialized but the American Museum of Natural History in New York City and others often honor youthful site spotters and finders of mammoth fossils. Several turned up in response to the amateur survey but the national champion must surely be an Arkansas Archæological Society member, John Newton of Russellville, who recorded sixty sites for his state survey the summer before entering Arkansas Tech and was still hard at it as a sophomore in 1962!

Even those who live in urban or suburban areas can play this game. Construction of big buildings, streets, highways, shopping centers, and community air raid shelters often means valuable evidence may be uncovered. Watch your newspapers; be on the spot; keep your eyes open; question workmen — with luck, you may spot something. If so, *report it at once.*

If no action is taken by the professionals and there is not a moment to lose, you might try to salvage something on your own. But *watch your step,* this could prove dangerous, and you will need the foreman's friendly cooperation. Then take the advice of a museum man who likes to tell young people, "Dig with a teaspoon and a camel's hair brush, not a bulldozer and a steam shovel. And make it a rule to photograph it before you pick it up."

As for digging otherwise on your own, better stick to your own backyard. There is a federal law protecting antiquities, and many states have laws, too, covering all public lands. For digging on private property, you must, of course, get the owner's permission.

Many amateurs begin as collectors but most of them these days outgrow the habit. As their horizons expand, they become more interested in the "man behind the artifact" than in the thing itself. Besides, in the light of what organized amateurs are accomplishing today in America, doesn't collecting seem a bit tame and old-fashioned?

"It is essential to realize that all archæology is one. The fact that it is a work containing many chapters does not mean that it can be broken up."

— *Philippe Diolé*

In order to see our planet as it actually is — a sphere revolving in space — you must look at a three-dimensional globe instead of a map printed on a flat surface It is the same way with archæology, a three-dimensional human activity defying the barriers of time and space. To be understood at all, it must be looked at in the round. So spin the globe and see where your finger lands.

EGYPT? Exciting things are always happening here.

In Nubia, an international corps of archaeologists, under UNESCO sponsorship, engaged in a mighty salvage project, rather reminiscent of our own River Basin Program.

The construction of the High Dam at Aswan, as a solution to current water problems, means that the rising waters of the Nile now engulf and cover several of the great temples that are the heritage of Ancient Egypt — some of these monuments were saved. As with our own project, some of the treasures had been sacrificed after they had been recorded in words and pictures; others were saved.

The greatest challenge was offered by the Abu Simbil Temples, miraculously carved from red sandstone cliffs along the Nile by order of Rameses II in the thirteenth century, B.C. The great temple, with a 107-foot-high facade, has four huge colossi guarding the entrance to nine engraved and painted chambers. The smaller temple, dedicated to Rameses' Queen Nefretiry is, in its way, as exquisite a memorial as India's Taj Mahal.

Engineers of many nationalities drafted plans to save Abu Simbil. At first, the Italian proposal of lifting each temple in one piece was favored, but this turned out to be too costly. Instead Egypt and UNESCO decided upon a plan for cutting up the temple in as large segments as possible and reassembling them, as with a jigsaw puzzle, 200 feet above the river at flood level.

Italconsult; UNESCO Courier

Abu Simbil Temple, the 250,000-ton ancient structure.

In 1923, Egyptian archæology caught the world's imagination when Howard Carter, a student of the famed egyptologist, Sir Flinders Petrie, and his wealthy patron, Lord Carnarvon, discovered the golden treasures of Tutankhamen's tomb. "King Tut," as he was soon nicknamed by Americans, had been a minor boy pharaoh of the Eighteenth Dynasty. Presumably, Tutankhamen began his journey to the next life less lavishly equipped than some other important personages. At any rate his tomb's innermost chamber had somehow escaped the attention of grave robbers, those most tireless of all diggers. When Carter's long and patient search ended so gloriously, he found the seals still unbroken on the portal of the tomb, the beautiful quartzite sarcophagus encasing the mummy, and all the inner chamber's breathtaking riches untouched — except by the hand of time. For once the early Egyptians' many forms of "burglar insurance," namely top secret burial plans, superstitious fear of myriad gods and priests, labyrinthine passages, "booby traps," and false doors, had foiled the greedy ghouls who have burrowed in the sands from time immemorial.

So you spin the globe again, and your finger lands — where?

ITALY . . . this is the very fountainhead of archæology, and nowhere more than along the Bay of Naples in the shadow of still smoldering Vesuvius. It was an ill wind from the Northwest that blew deathly volcanic ash, sulphuric fumes, and a pounding rain of pumice stone over the star-crossed city of Pompeii one August afternoon in A.D. 79. But that same wind was to bring archæology the greatest gift it has ever received. This sophisticated little city, where 2,000 men, women, and children perished in agony as they tried to escape through the city gates, or sought shelter in the cellars of their homes, has found "resurrection" through the magic of the spade. Almost continuously since the accidental discovery of this site in the middle of the eighteenth century, excavations have been carried on, and the work of uncovering and restoring these ruins will continue for many decades to come.

Pompeii and its smaller, more rustic neighbor, Herculaneum — victim of the same eruption of Vesuvius — are unique because rather than being destroyed by the ravages of time or war, they were preserved beneath a protective natural layer (like plants under a blanket of snow). When this is removed, a poignant glimpse of a long-dead people, interrupted in the midst of their everyday activities, is revealed to the wondering eyes of the living.

Not only archæologists are fascinated by this phenomenon. Ever since Queen Victoria's period, when Lord Bulwer-Lytton wrote his best seller, The Last Days of Pompeii, tourists have flocked here. In the "treasure hunt" days, Pompeii was treated like a quarry, full of beautiful, valuable, and sometimes very curious works of art. But, as the world's longest continuous dig, it has, inevitably, reflected increasingly scientific trends; and today the full potential of this opportunity to step back into the past is being realized.

Since modern equipment makes it easier to dig deeper — as far down as forty feet — through the solidified volcanic mud, progress at Pompeii has been accelerated in recent years. But Herculaneum buried still deeper under tufa or lava had a late start. Little, in fact, could be accomplished there before

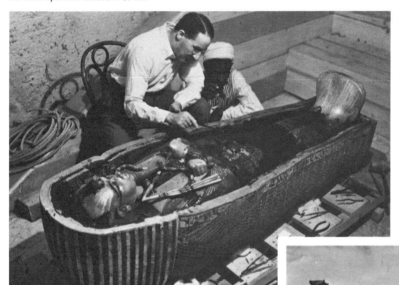

With a native assistant, Howard Carter examines the
gold innermost coffin of King Tut.

The temple of Apollo, with Vesuvius as a backdrop,
symbolizes the eternal drama of Pompeii.

the 1930's. By following the town plans, archæologists methodically dig up
Pompeii *insula by insula,* or quarter by quarter, with occasional side excursions to the fashionable suburban villas where many prominent Romans spent
their summers. Furnishings of the public and private buildings are left intact
and the facades, sometimes two stories high, are cleverly restored. The uncanny effect of a street, whose rightful occupants may return at any moment,
is heightened by the Pompeiians' wonderfully human habit of scrawling advertisements and personal comments in Latin on the walls. As one travel
writer says, you seem to be hearing echoes of the thousand voices of the city.

As at Colonial Williamsburg in Virginia across the seas, you find here
in Italy the new focus of archæological attention on the way ordinary people,
not just the ruling classes, lived, worked, and had their being.

Next stop: MEXICO.

As romantically mysterious as any site in the Old World, is the Sacred Well or Cenote of Chichén-Itzá in Yucatan where the Maya cast beautiful maidens, golden and copper bells, and beads of crystal, jade, and pearl as sacrifices to their gods!

The riddle of this haunted spot is part of the riddle of the Maya themselves, a tribe that reached a remarkably high state of civilization 2,000 years ago. When the Conquistadores arrived from Spain in the sixteenth century, these Indians had disappeared, leaving only the ruins of their great cities and temples as staggering as the Egyptian pyramids, abandoned to the spreading jungle.

A pioneering and perilous experiment to solve the riddle by diving into the Cenote's murky depths was made in the 1880's by Edward Herbert Thompson, an amateur archæologist. By coincidence, both Thompson and his predecessor the Mayan scholar and explorer John Lloyd Stephens were U.S. consular officers. Even with the primitive diving equipment of his day, Thompson, in the course of four years, was able to deliver a remarkable collection of artifacts to his backers at the Peabody Museum of Harvard.

In 1960, in line with the modern practice of sharing archæological finds with the country of their origin, Harvard University presented almost 100 of these treasures to the Mexican National Institute of Anthropology and History. The following year Mexican divers and archæologists performed a twentieth-century version of Thompson's experiment. This expedition, aided by the National Geographic Society, used not only frogman equipment but a variation of the airlift, devised by Edwin Link for his famous underwater salvage work at Port Royal, Jamaica.

Among the first Mayan treasures brought up from Chichén-Itzá's Sacred Well were these gold figurines typical of their mysterious makers' workmanship.

Peabody Museum,
Harvard University

All the equipment had to be lowered eighty feet by derrick from the rim of the well, which is really a sinkhole surrounded by limestone cliffs, to the surface of the water. Here a raft was floated on steel drums, with the airlift's big pipe going through a hole in the middle. As the water drawn from the bottom gushed forth, it was sieved, just like soil at a regular dig. Among the thousands of finds retrieved by this method and the more customary diving technique were the familiar little sacred bells, beads, copal incense burners and curious crude rubber or latex effigies of Mayan workmanship.

A more important result, however, was the first opportunity to make maps and diagrams of the bottom. Instead of planning more underwater salvage, archæologists are hoping that hydraulic engineers will someday drain the Cenote so they can really excavate this significant site.

Meanwhile, more secrets of the Maya are expected to be revealed by a Mexican Institute-National Geographic team now exploring a maze of underground chambers at a cave near Chichén-Itzá known as the Temple of the Jaguar's Throne.

It may be a small world, but it will take us a long while to get around it at this rate! So let's spin the globe faster and look quickly at some oddities reported from here and there.

In SPAIN, archaeology tied up Barcelona traffic and entertained "sidewalk superintendents" as the remains of the Roman city wall are excavated. "It's a noisy dig," said one archaeologist, "with pneumatic drills yammering away most of the time."

In COLORADO, amateur collectors of Indian artifacts, rocks, semiprecious stones, and petrified wood in the Rocky Mountain area hold a large exhibition each September. It has been incorporated as The Original Loveland Stone Age Fair of the World.

In ISRAEL, a British and Israeli team investigated the *real* King Solomon's (copper) mines — Rider Haggard's King Solomon's (diamond) mines in Africa are only imaginary!

In ENGLAND, archaeologists conducted experiments to discover how men without machinery transported the huge blocks (known as *sarsens* and *bluestones*) to construct their mysterious Stonehenge. A workman was heard to remark, "Reckon it was done with blood, sweat, tears, and brute force."

In TEXAS, the Humble Oil and Refining Company changed plans for the location of a new well near Houston because diggers (industrial not scientific) found interesting Indian artifacts on the original site chosen. When archæologists put *their* spades to work, four skeletons were unearthed from what is believed to have been a burial ground of the Wintun tribe in A.D. 500. Perhaps Humble is so archæology minded because its enterprises include a carbon-14 dating laboratory.

In SWEDEN, the 300-year-old warship "Vasa," which sank outside the royal harbor on the day it was launched, under went a dehydrating treatment in dry dock while scholars study, and museum workers prepare for display everything found on board from sailor's slippers to bronze cannon. Admiralty Engineer Anders Franzen fulfilled a boyhood dream when he found it 110 feet down in muck which one diver called "oatmeal."

In JUDEA, archæologists are still finding scrolls and documents in caves but some of them are a far cry from the Dead Sea variety which caused such ferment among Christian and Jewish theologians fifteen years ago. The first papyri translated in a bundle of forty from one desert cave included a marriage contract, a lease of a palm grove, and a widow's request for money from her son's guardians.

In GUATEMALA, archaeologists have been helped in the study of ancient Maya hieroglyphs, thanks to the discovery at Tikal of a more than 1,500-year-old great stone (stela) such as was erected outside temples. All the others have been badly eroded by the weather, but this broken one was, for some reason, safely stored away in a back room.

In DENMARK, Dr. Ole Klindt-Jensen has designed a Quonset hut type "excavation house" of wood and transparent plastic which he can set up in an hour over his digs at Bornholm Island. At night he packs it away on top of the bus which he uses for lunch breaks and lab work as well as commuting.

In IRAN, 400-foot Marlik Mound in the Goha Valley has been nicknamed locally, "The Mound That Lays Golden Eggs." Rich finds are being made there by Iranian archæologist Ezat Negahban.

In MASSACHUSETTS, noted amateur Roland W. Robbins, specialist in lesser-known historic sites, has unearthed the Duxbury home of the Longfellow hero and heroine, John and Priscilla Alden, at the request of their 300 descendants, all members of the Alden Kindred Association.

In RUSSIA, a medieval site yielded a letter from a man dunning his brother for the repayment of a loan. It was inscribed on birchbark in American Indian fashion!

In NEW MEXICO, at White Sands Missile Range, Sp4 Laurens Hammack, an MP, has found many artifacts, including pottery of the Pueblo type. Other GI's and officers, including Brig. Gen. John G. Shinkle in command at White Sands, have assisted Hammack.

Somewhere in the Pacific — as they said in wartime — Roger S. Duff of the Canterbury Museum, Christchurch, N.Z. was following the trail of a type of stone adz as tracer for the Peruvian migrations to Polynesia. His eventual purpose was to test the South American migration theories of Thor Heyerdahl so familiar to readers of the best seller, *Kon-Tiki.*

The cold waters of the Baltic Sea preserved in remarkable condition the timbers of the 17th-century "Vasa" whose stern was photographed in drydock at Stockholm.

Peat bogs preserved, in exceptionally good condition, this head of Tollund man who lived in Denmark 2,000 years ago. This find salvaged in 1950 was dated by means of pollen analysis.

Only reproductions remain of the mysterious, magnificent Golden Horns of prehistoric Denmark. The originals, discovered a century or two before, were stolen from the Royal Museum at Copenhagen in 1802.

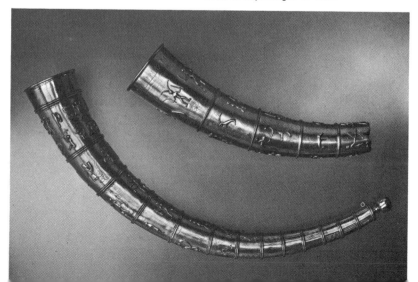

"The plainest reason for the study of history . . . is simply to satisfy

natural curiosity — to give the pleasure that all men know in finding

out about something, whether birds, or batting averages, the work-

ings of an engine, or of a universe."

— *Herbert J. Muller*

Young people are lucky, they'll be present when the next installment of Man's history comes out! Very few members of any generation have the opportunity to make history themselves, or to affect the progress of the sciences or the arts. However, if science and art are a way of thinking, a way of looking at things, then everyone of us has the opportunity to keep score and to be fully *aware* of what is happening. We can even learn, by degrees, to appreciate intellectually something that makes us uncomfortable physically. How? By keeping the arrowhead of curiosity sharp and ready for lifetime use.

When it was first announced that the United States was planning a satellite, it was revealing to compare the reactions of the older and younger generations. Older people, probably more puzzled and disturbed than they would admit, groaned, "What next!" and added space to their long list of adult worries. Their sons and daughters, on the other hand, were excited but not shocked. If they were science minded — or perhaps just science-fiction readers — they were prepared for such wonders. If they were puzzled, they started looking for answers. If they said, "What next?" they meant it. They were already thinking in terms of interplanetary travel.

The study of the past has a future, too; we have hardly scratched the surface. In the next installment our modern scientific devices will seem primitive; they will long since have been replaced with better things. One of them might even be discovered in a decade or two by a reader of this book. Stranger things have happened.

What is the big lesson to be learned from the River Basin Program and other salvage projects? Not just the fact that the evidence of our past is being destroyed and should be saved, although that is something well worth remembering. But basically it is the demonstration of what archæologists can accomplish when they are given a sense of urgency, *plus money, manpower and a coordinated and imaginative program.*

Money: Several foreign governments, including the Soviet, are fully aware of the patriotic and economic importance of preservation of their historic and prehistoric sites. They make generous allowance for archæology in their budgets. Aside from government subsidies, which may or may not be the answer for the United States problem, archæology of our own Indian and historic sites could certainly use more private financing from foundations, individuals, and major industries. Most of the burden today is carried by universities and museums, and a large proportion of these funds is expended abroad.

Manpower: This is a big problem which is also partly financial since the training required for a professional archæologist is not only arduous and

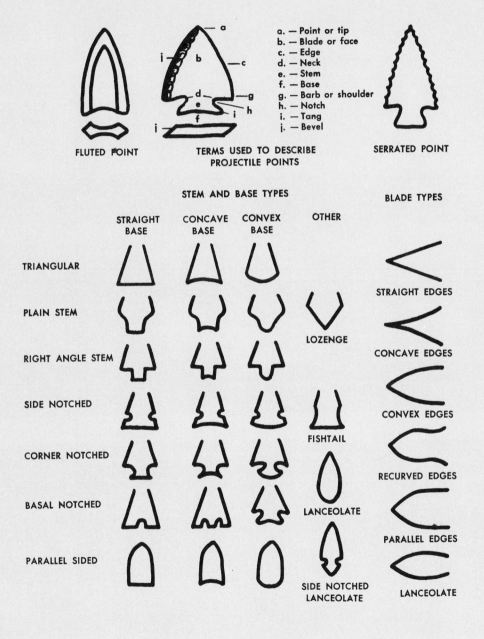

a. — Point or tip
b. — Blade or face
c. — Edge
d. — Neck
e. — Stem
f. — Base
g. — Barb or shoulder
h. — Notch
i. — Tang
j. — Bevel

FLUTED POINT

TERMS USED TO DESCRIBE
PROJECTILE POINTS

SERRATED POINT

STEM AND BASE TYPES

BLADE TYPES

STRAIGHT BASE   CONCAVE BASE   CONVEX BASE   OTHER

TRIANGULAR

STRAIGHT EDGES

PLAIN STEM

LOZENGE

CONCAVE EDGES

RIGHT ANGLE STEM

CONVEX EDGES

SIDE NOTCHED

FISHTAIL

CORNER NOTCHED

RECURVED EDGES

LANCEOLATE

BASAL NOTCHED

PARALLEL EDGES

PARALLEL SIDED

SIDE NOTCHED
LANCEOLATE

LANCEOLATE

41

INDIAN TRIBES of the UNITED STATES
EXCLUDING ALASKA

The various Indian tribes are shown where they were located during the period of their greatest significance in American history.

MICMAC
MALECITE
PENOBSCOT
ABNAKI
PENNACOOK
MASSACHUSET
NARRAGANSET
PEQUOT
MONTAUK
MAHICAN
MOHAWK
DELAWARE
NANTICOKE
SECOTAN
ONEIDA
ONONDAGA
CAYUGA
SENECA
SUSQUE HANNA
CONOY
POWHATAN
MONACAN
TUSCARORA
TUTELO
MONETON
MONACAN
TOBACCO
NEUTRALS
ERIE
BLACK MINQUA
CATAWBA
CUSABO
AIS
YAMASI
TEQUESTA
TIMUCUA
SEMINOLES
CALUSA
CHEROKEE
YUCHI
CREEK
APPALACHEE
SEMINOLES
HURON
OTTAWA
CHIPPEWA
MENOMINEE
WINNEBAGO
POTAWATOMI
MIAMI
MOSOPELEA
SHAWNEE
CHICKASAW
CHOCTAW
MOBILE
BILOXI
NATCHEZ
TUNICA
CHITIMACHA
ATTACAPA
KARANKAWA
SAUK & FOX
KICKAPOO
ILLINOIS
MISSOURI
QUAPAW
CADDO
CHIPPEWA
SIOUX
IOWA
OTO
OMAHA
KANSA (KAW)
OSAGE
WICHITA
TONKAWA
COAHUILTEC
HIDATSA
ASSINIBOINE
MANDAN
ARIKARA
PONCA
PAWNEE
CHEYENNE
KIOWA
COMANCHE
APACHE
ATSINA (GROS VENTRES)
CROW
CHEYENNE
ARAPAHO
CHEYENNE
APACHE
KERES
TANO
ZUÑI
APACHE
BLACKFEET
KOOTENAI
FLATHEAD
COEUR D'ALENE
SHOSHONE
UTE
NAVAHO
HOPI
YAVAPAI
PIMA
PAPAGO
COLUMBIA
CAYUSE
NEZ PERCE
PALOOS
BANNOCK
SHOSHONE
PAIUTE
HUALAPAI
CHEMEHUEVI
YUMA
MARICOPA
SERRANO
DIEGUEÑO
GABRIELINO
NISQUALI
YAKIMA
KLAMATH
MODOC
MONO
CHUMASH
NOOTKA
QUINAULT
CHINOOK
KALAPUYA
YUROK
SHASTA
YANA
WINTUN
MAIDU
MIWOK
YOKUTS
COSTAÑO
SALINA
POMO
PAIUTE

A successful search for an 8,000-year-old mastodon's skeleton was sparked by two Hackensack (N.J.) boys digging up a pair of its teeth. Advising them is George Whitaker, an American Museum of Natural History staff paleontologist.

lengthy but expensive. More undergraduate scholarships, in addition to graduate fellowships and grants, seem to be desirable. Long-range recruitment is another possibility.

Elementary courses in anthropology in secondary schools are one answer. So far no one but the outstanding American anthropologist, Ashley Montagu, seems to feel that it should be emphasized throughout the entire educational system. Some science teachers manage to slant their courses in that direction like Herbert C. Kraft, curator of the museum of Seton Hall University, South Orange, N. J.

While teaching in an Elizabeth, N. J. elementary school a few years ago, Mr. Kraft encouraged his pupils to settle their views over Neanderthal Man by writing personally to experts including Dr. Montagu, Carlton Coon, and the director of the British Museum. The result was that they received interested, friendly, and enlightening answers. The experts differed in their views — but that in itself was a lesson worth learning.

A few other schools are encouraging study in related fields and scheduling classes in archæology. Verde Valley, a progressive coeducational boarding school in Arizona, has lively classes and field trips which make anthropology a favorite course. Students visit Navajo and Hopi reservations; sometimes live briefly in Indian homes and, during spring vacation, take a tour by truck to famous sites in Mexico.

Paleontology is tops in popularity at the Webb School of California although it is an extracurricular activity there. The boys are great fossil hunters and, over the years, their weekend field trips in the vicinity, and trips to other states during vacation, have furnished a fossil collection for the school's private museum. This collection has become nationally known. Several of the boys obtained advanced degrees and one, Malcolm McKenna, is a curator at the American Museum of Natural History, New York City.

Trips to great European sites and centers are incentives to an archæological career besides being exciting experiences. Student tours to these spots have been sponsored by educational groups.

Coordinated, imaginative program: Could we not someday achieve an institution devoted to collating and coordinating the research of specialists in the fields of archæology, anthropology, and ethnology? If their learning could be pooled; if they could study past civilizations, primitive peoples, ancient and living; or if such broad and vital long-range subjects as "The Effects of Diet on Man," or "The Effects of Climate on Man," could be studied, think what progress could be achieved!

Under the same roof and ready to assist their brother scientists in time-saving research, would be paleontologists, geologists, zoologists, chemists, physicists, and botanists. Impossible? What about the Manhattan Project?

Some morning your paper may report a new dicovery that sets the clock of Man's life on earth millions of years farther back than today's estimates, or you may be told that the Amerinds came here long before the last inter-glacial period and weren't Mongoloid after all!

You may read of the discovery of lost cities like Atlantis; of whole civilizations brought to light because man has learned to dig deeper, interpret his clues better, explore unlikely and inaccessible areas. There may be discoveries under the Arctic ice, in the Gulf of Mexico, in the caverns of those mysterious underground rivers or siphons in France, or perhaps in some obscure cave in Kentucky that only small boys are foolhardy enough to enter!

So remember those young amateurs in New Mexico who feel challenged to ask questions and then look for answers. Also remember that all great discoveries are made by people with vision to question what everybody else accepts, and the perseverence and ability to find new answers. Maybe not the final answers, but one step forward.

This monument with runic inscriptions, probably a milestone of early Viking voyages, is from the Runestone Museum, Alexandria, Minn.

Runestone Museum, Alexandria, Minn.

Mayan pottery toy representing an alligator

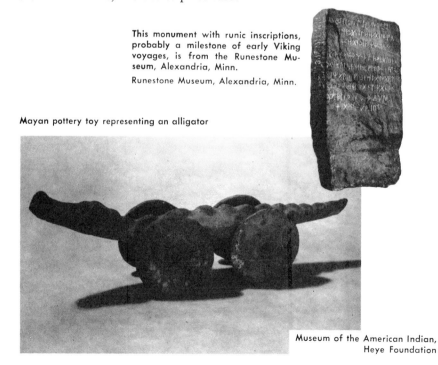

Museum of the American Indian,
Heye Foundation

One generation's pet theories are examined skeptically by the next generation, then modified, perhaps at last discarded. It happens in other sciences, as well as archæology. Next time you see one of those theories labeled *"true"* ask yourself *"— or false?"* and think it over for a while. Then do some serious research before you decide.

That goes not only for theories about big problems like Man's origins and migrations, but explanations for "Why primitive peoples did or do such funny things." Try to see if you can work out a normal, human reason, looking at it from their point of view. There usually is one — or more, and often you can find something quite like it in our own society. For instance, weren't the Indians too mature for such a Halloween gesture as wearing warpaint to frighten their enemies? Could it have filled the same function as a modern soldier's ribbons which he wears while keeping his medals at home? Those headdresses of coup feathers were too beautiful and hard to make to risk on any but ceremonial occasions.

As an anthropology instructor, Zdenek Salzmann, tells his Verde Valley classes, "If we wish to look at other peoples as weird, then we must also reconcile ourselves to appearing equally weird to them. Mightn't it be more reasonable, though, to take others seriously and then expect the like in return?"

So keep your curiosity sharp as an arrowhead and be ready to read the next installment in the world's most exciting mystery story that will appear as long as there is a Last Man on this planet. Should you be one of the happy few chosen to write a word or two of that installment, congratulations and good digging to you!

Lenni Lenape Stone

ARCHAEOLOGY QUIZ

1. Did one of the Stone Age beasts, the hairy mammoth, look something like this?
2. Were these "bannerstones" used as sinkers by Indian fishermen?
3. What was the significance of Indian "effigy mounds" like the Great Serpent in Ohio?
4. Did Indians make "birdstones" as ritual objects, art forms, toys or . . . ?
5. Could this 2,000-year-old Greek stone disc actually be a primitive computer?

THE SCIENCE-HOBBY SERIES

1.

2.

3.

4.

5.

Where to Write

NOTE: Some State Societies have no permanent headquarters so the best way to make contact may be through museums or the anthropology department of universities. If your state is not listed here, consult the achnowledgements.

Alabama: State Archæological Society, Mound State Monument Museum, Moundville

Arizona: State Archæological Society, State Museum, Tucson

California: Lowie Museum of Anthropology, State University, Berkeley

Connecticut: State Historical Society, Hartford

Delaware: State Archæological Society, State Museum, Dover

Florida: State Anthropological Society, State Museum, Gainesville

Idaho: State Historical Society, Boise

Illinois: State Archæological Society, Natural History Museum, Chicago

Kentucky: State University Museum, Lexington

Maine: State Archæological Society, Robert Abbe Museum of Stone Age Antiquities, Bar Harbor

Maryland: State Archæological Society, Academy of Sciences, Baltimore

Michigan: State Archæological Society, Kelsey Museum, State University, Ann Arbor

Minnesota: State Archæological Society, Minneapolis Public Library, Minneapolis

Mississippi: State University Museum, University

Nebraska: State Historical Society, Lincoln

Nevada: State Museum, Carson City

New Hampshire: State Archæological Society, Dartmouth College Museum, Hanover

Ohio: State Historical Society, State Museum, Columbus

Oklahoma: State Anthropological Society, State University, Norman

Oregon: State Historical Society, Portland

Pennsylvania: Society for Pennsylvania Archæology, Carnegie Museum, Pittsburgh

Rhode Island: State Archæological Society, Brown University Museum, Providence

South Carolina: State Archæological Society, Charleston Museum Charleston

Vermont: State Historical Society, State Library, Montpelier

Virginia: State Archæological Society, State University, Charlottesville

Washington: State Archæological Society, State University, Seattle

West Virginia: State Archæological Society, Mound Museum, Moundsville

Wyoming: State Museum, Cheyenne

We specialize in publishing quality books for young people. For a complete list please write

LERNER PUBLICATIONS COMPANY

241 First Avenue North, Minneapolis, Minnesota 55401